Maitland

by Iain Gray

Lang**Syne**
PUBLISHING
WRITING *to* REMEMBER

LangSyne
PUBLISHING
WRITING *to* REMEMBER

79 Main Street, Newtongrange,
Midlothian EH22 4NA
Tel: 0131 344 0414   Fax: 0845 075 6085
E-mail: info@lang-syne.co.uk
www.langsyneshop.co.uk

Design by Dorothy Meikle
Printed by Printwell Ltd
© Lang Syne Publishers Ltd 2021

All rights reserved. No part of this publication may be reproduced, stored or introduced into a retrieval system, or transmitted in any form or by any means (electronic, mechanical, photocopying, recording or otherwise) without the prior written permission of Lang Syne Publishers Ltd.

ISBN 978-1-85217-788-1

Maitland

MOTTO:
By wisdom and courage

CREST:
A lion, ducally crowned, holding a sword in its right paw and a fleur-de-lis in the left

TERRITORIES:
The Borders and East Lothian

NAME variations include:
Matland
Maltland
Matlain

Chapter one:

The origins of the clan system

by Rennie McOwan

The original Scottish clans of the Highlands and the great families of the Lowlands and Borders were gatherings of families, relatives, allies and neighbours for mutual protection against rivals or invaders.

Scotland experienced invasion from the Vikings, the Romans and English armies from the south. The Norman invasion of what is now England also had an influence on land-holding in Scotland. Some of these invaders stayed on and in time became 'Scottish'.

The word clan derives from the Gaelic language term 'clann', meaning children, and it was first used many centuries ago as communities were formed around tribal lands in glens and mountain fastnesses.

The format of clans changed over the centuries, but at its best the chief and his family held the land on behalf of all, like trustees, and the ordinary clansmen and women believed they had a blood relationship with the founder of their clan.

There were two way duties and obligations. An inadequate chief could be deposed and replaced by someone of greater ability.

Clan people had an immense pride in race. Their relationship with the chief was like adult children to a father and they had a real dignity.

The concept of clanship is very old and a more feudal notion of authority gradually crept in.

Pictland, for instance, was divided into seven principalities ruled by feudal leaders who were the strongest and most charismatic leaders of their particular groups.

By the sixth century the 'British' kingdoms of Strathclyde, Lothian and Celtic Dalriada (Argyll) had emerged and Scotland, as one nation, began to take shape in the time of King Kenneth MacAlpin.

Some chiefs claimed descent from ancient kings which may not have been accurate in every case.

By the twelfth and thirteenth centuries the clans and families were more strongly brought under the central control of Scottish monarchs.

Lands were awarded and administered more and more under royal favour, yet the power of the area clan chiefs was still very great.

The long wars to ensure Scotland's

independence against the expansionist ideas of English monarchs extended the influence of some clans and reduced the lands of others.

Those who supported Scotland's greatest king, Robert the Bruce, were awarded the territories of the families who had opposed his claim to the Scottish throne.

In the Scottish Borders country – the notorious Debatable Lands – the great families built up a ferocious reputation for providing warlike men accustomed to raiding into England and occasionally fighting one another.

Chiefs had the power to dispense justice and to confiscate lands and clan warfare produced a society where martial virtues – courage, hardiness, tenacity – were greatly admired.

Gradually the relationship between the clans and the Crown became strained as Scottish monarchs became more orientated to life in the Lowlands and, on occasion, towards England.

The Highland clans spoke a different language, Gaelic, whereas the language of Lowland Scotland and the court was Scots and in more modern times, English.

Highlanders dressed differently, had different

customs, and their wild mountain land sometimes seemed almost foreign to people living in the Lowlands.

It must be emphasised that Gaelic culture was very rich and story-telling, poetry, piping, the clarsach (harp) and other music all flourished and were greatly respected.

Highland culture was different from other parts of Scotland but it was not inferior or less sophisticated.

Central Government, whether in London or Edinburgh, sometimes saw the Gaelic clans as a challenge to their authority and some sent expeditions into the Highlands and west to crush the power of the Lords of the Isles.

Nevertheless, when the eighteenth century Jacobite Risings came along the cause of the Stuarts was mainly supported by Highland clans.

The word Jacobite comes from the Latin for James – Jacobus. The Jacobites wanted to restore the exiled Stuarts to the throne of Britain.

The monarchies of Scotland and England became one in 1603 when King James VI of Scotland (1st of England) gained the English throne after Queen Elizabeth died.

The Union of Parliaments of Scotland and England, the Treaty of Union, took place in 1707.

Some Highland clans, of course, and Lowland families opposed the Jacobites and supported the incoming Hanoverians.

After the Jacobite cause finally went down at Culloden in 1746 a kind of ethnic cleansing took place. The power of the chiefs was curtailed. Tartan and the pipes were banned in law.

Many emigrated, some because they wanted to, some because they were evicted by force. In addition, many Highlanders left for the cities of the south to seek work.

Many of the clan lands became home to sheep and deer shooting estates.

But the warlike traditions of the clans and the great Lowland and Border families lived on, with their descendants fighting bravely for freedom in two world wars.

Remember the men from whence you came, says the Gaelic proverb, and to that could be added the role of many heroic women.

The spirit of the clan, of having roots, whether Highland or Lowland, means much to thousands of people.

Meanwhile, many families proudly boast the heraldic device known as a Coat of Arms,.

The central motif of the Coat of Arms would originally have been what was sometimes borne on the shield of a warrior to distinguish himself from others on the battlefield.

Clan warfare produced a society where courage and tenacity were greatly admired

Chapter two:

Politics and poetry

From affairs of high state to the judiciary and politics, bearers of the Maitland name have stamped an indelible mark on the pages of the turbulent drama that is Scotland's history, accruing high honours and distinction along the way.

Originally a nickname, it stems from the French 'mautalent' or 'maltent', indicating 'bad tempered.'

This, in turn, comes from the Latin 'malum', indicating 'bad', while another colourful possibility is that it means 'evil genius'.

Another more grisly theory, meanwhile, is that it derives from the Latin *quasi mutilates in bello* – meaning 'as if mutilated in war'.

A Clan Maitland tradition is that they trace their descent from a Norman knight who fought at the side of William the Conqueror at the battle of Hastings in 1066 and was rewarded with lands in Northumbria, in the far north of England.

Lending credence to this is that, in the now redundant form 'Matalant', a Thomas de (of)

Matalant was settled in the Scottish Borders, in Berwickshire, during the reign from 1165 to 1214 of King William I, better known to posterity as William the Lion.

Nearly 100 years earlier, trouble had brewed for the Conqueror in the far northern reaches of his realm where those who would come to take the Maitland name had settled – with rebellions stirred by Edgar Atheling, claimant to the former kingdom of Wessex.

In 'The Harrying of the North', William's response was brutal – laying waste from 1069 to 1070 to the northern shires, including the city of York and replacing native aristocracy and their followers – such as those who would come to bear the Maitland name in Scotland – with Normans deemed more loyal.

In 1071, King Malcolm III of Scotland married Margaret, a sister of the Saxon Edgar Atheling and therefore had an affinity with the dispossessed northerners such as those who would come to take the Maitland name – welcoming them to settle in his kingdom.

It is possible that the first of them were part of this exodus from Northumbria, with their descendants becoming so entrenched they were considered important enough to be the subject of record, as was Sir Thomas de Matalant in the late twelfth century.

It was not until about the middle of the fourteenth century, meanwhile, that 'Maitland' became the standardised spelling of the name – with a confusing number of variations including 'Matalant' and 'Mautlant' appearing on record up until then.

For the sake of clarity and consistency, 'Maitland' is therefore the form adopted for the remainder of this narrative history of what became Clan Maitland.

They thrived in their new Borders heartland – with Sir Richard Maitland acquiring lands including Thirlestane, near Lauder, through his marriage to Avicia, heiress of Sir Thomas de Thirlestane – during the reign from 1249 to 1286 of King Alexander III.

The clan first steps fully onto the pages of the nation's story during the First War of Scottish Independence of 1296 to 1328, with Sir William Maitland ardent in his support of Robert the Bruce and present with the great warrior king at his victory on the field of Bannockburn in midsummer of 1314.

Sir William was succeeded in his lands and title by his son Sir Robert Maitland, who also acquired the lands of Lethington, near Haddington, East Lothian, while one of his three sons, also named Robert, was the ancestor of an Aberdeenshire branch of the clan whose seat was at Balhargardy, near Inverurie.

But lands and titles often came at a heavy price – to be paid for on the battlefield.

A descendant of Sir William Maitland who had fought at Bannockburn, and who also shared his name, was among the 5,000 Scots including King James IV, an archbishop, two bishops, eleven earls, fifteen barons, and 300 knights killed at the battle of Flodden in 1513.

The king had embarked on the venture after Queen Anne of France, under the terms of the Auld Alliance between Scotland and her nation, appealed to him to 'break a lance' on her behalf and act as her chosen knight.

Crossing the border into England at the head of a 25,000-strong army, James engaged an English force numbering 20,000 and commanded by the Earl of Surrey.

Despite their numerical superiority and bravery, however, the Scots proved no match for the skilled English artillery and superior military tactics of Surrey – with Maitland among the 300 knights who fell.

His son and heir Sir Richard Maitland of Lethington and Thirlestane served his country not on the battlefield but through high state office, while he was also a noted poet.

Born in 1496 and a Senator of the College of Justice and Lord of Session, he served as Keeper of the Great Seal of Scotland and also of the Privy Seal while, despite suffering from deteriorating eyesight and eventually going blind, wrote histories and poetry while also collecting works by others.

These were collated into the *Maitland Manuscripts*, recognised as an important source of Scottish literature of the fifteenth and sixteenth centuries and now held by the Pepys Library of Magdalene College, University of Cambridge.

He died in 1586, while through his marriage to Mariotta Cranstoun, daughter of Sir Thomas Cranstoun of Corsbie, Berwickshire, he was the father of two sons and three daughters.

One of these daughters, Mary Maitland, born in about 1550 and who died in 1596, followed in her father's footsteps as a poet, while also fulfilling the important function of transcribing much of his work as his sight deteriorated – recording and preserving what became the *Maitland Manuscripts*.

Her elder brother was the politician and diplomat William Maitland of Lethington who, known as 'Secretary Lethington' played a key role in the troubled affairs of the ill-fated Mary Queen of Scots.

Born in 1525 and educated at the University of St Andrews, as Secretary of State to the queen until her enforced abdication in July of 1567 in favour of her son, James VI (James I of England), by a body known as the Confederate Lords, he had to steer a precarious course through the dangerous political and religious waters of his time.

His knowledge of foreign, particularly English, politics made him invaluable to Mary and he served for a time as ambassador to the court of her cousin Queen Elizabeth.

Implicated in the murder in 1566 of Mary's private secretary David Rizzio – who had been the subject of what appear to have been entirely baseless rumours he was her secret lover – he understandably fell from favour for a time, but rallied to her cause following her capture by the Lords of the Congregation at the battle of Carberry Hill in July of 1567.

She escaped confinement but, on May 23,

1568, forces loyal to her under the command of the Earl of Argyll were routed at the battle of Langside, near Glasgow, and she fled into what she then naively thought would be the protection of Queen Elizabeth.

She was instead fated to be held under close guard in a succession of strongholds before her execution on February 8, 1587, in the Great Hall of Fotheringhay Castle, in Northamptonshire.

Following her flight from Scotland, meanwhile, Maitland had acted in her interests and formed a party with the avowed aim of restoring her to power.

But his intrigues led to his arrest in 1569 and, following further political upheaval that resulted in the execution in May of 1573 of Sir William Kirkcaldy of Grange and his brother, also leading adherents of Mary's cause, Maitland died in prison a month later.

Through his marriage to Mary Fleming who, along with Mary Seaton, Mary Beaton and Mary Carmichael was one of the 'Four Marys' who accompanied Mary Queen of Scots to France in 1548 as her attendants, William Maitland of Lethington was the father of Margaret Maitland, who married Robert Ker, 1st Earl of Roxburgh.

Chapter three:

For King and country

Whether through marriage, as in the case of Margaret Maitland, or service to the state, the Maitlands continued to accrue high honours, lands and distinction – in particular John Maitland, 1st Duke and 2nd Earl of Lauderdale and 3rd Lord Thirlestane.

Born at Lethington in 1616, he was the eldest surviving son of John Maitland, 2nd Lord Maitland of Thirlestane, who was created Viscount of Lauderdale in the year of his son's birth and Earl of Lauderdale eight years later.

Destined to be at the very heart of matters of high state, adding to his illustrious pedigree was that his mother Lady Isabel Maitland was a daughter of Alexander Seton, 1st Earl of Dunfermline.

He came of age at a crucial time in the religious and political affairs of both Scotland and England through what became known as the Wars of the Three Kingdoms of Scotland, England and Ireland.

The conflict in Scotland had its origin in the

widely unpopular attempt by King Charles I to impose uniform religious practice between the Church of England and the proudly independent Scottish Kirk, through the introduction of the Episcopal Book of Common Prayer.

This led to widespread unrest and a momentous event occurred on February 28, 1638, with the signing of the *National Covenant* – a document as important to Scottish history as the equally famed *Declaration of Arbroath* of 1320.

Described as 'the glorious marriage day of the kingdom with God', the Covenant renounced Roman Catholic belief, pledged to uphold the Presbyterian religion and called for free parliaments and assemblies.

First signed at Edinburgh's Greyfriars Kirk by nobles, barons, burgesses and ministers, it was subscribed to the following day by hundreds of common folk.

Copies were made and dispatched around the nation and supported by thousands more – with its adherents becoming known as Covenanters and among them was John Maitland.

Civil war raged between Covenanters and Royalists in Scotland from 1638 until 1649, when

Charles I was beheaded on the orders of the English Parliament – whose military arm was the New Model Army under Oliver Cromwell.

Maitland's allegiance, in common with many other Scots, subsequently shifted to support for the ill-fated king's successor King Charles II, but defeat came at the battle of Worcester on September 1651.

Crushed by the New Model Army, about 3,000 Royalists were killed – while up to 8,000 Scottish prisoners were deported to the West Indies, Bermuda and New England to work as indentured labourers.

Among the prisoners was Maitland, who spent four years in captivity in England before being freed but his estates confiscated.

In the aftermath of the battle meanwhile, Charles II famously had to hide from his pursuers for a time in the branches of the 'royal oak' at Boscobel, Shropshire.

Escaping to the Continent, where he was joined in exile after his release from captivity by John Maitland, he returned to England on the Restoration of 1660.

Maitland had become a trusted adviser and close confidant of the king when in exile and, following the restoration, was rewarded with the powerful and lucrative appointment of Secretary of State for Scotland.

Exercising his almost dictatorial powers with relish, he was totally committed to the king's cause and was instrumental in the persecution of those Covenanters in whose ranks he had once stood.

So great did his grip on Scotland become that in 1669 he proudly declared: "The king is now master here in all causes and over all persons."

Created Duke of Lauderdale in 1672 and, two years later in the Peerage of England as Earl of Guilford and Baron Petersham, he became deeply unpopular not only in his native land but also in the English parliament and court circles.

This, combined with ill health, led to him resigning his posts two years before his death in 1682.

His first marriage had been to Lady Anne Home, daughter of Alexander Home, 1st Earl of Home and, following her death in 1672, his second to Elizabeth Murray, Countess of Dysart.

But having left no male heir, he was succeded in his Scottish earldom by his brother Charles Maitland as 3rd Earl of Lauderdale, while his dukedom and English titles became extinct.

A number of his descendants distinguished

themselves in service to the British state, in particular as Royal Navy officers.

Born in 1730, sixth son of Charles Maitland, 6th Earl of Lauderdale, Frederick Lewis Maitland served throughout conflicts including the Seven Years' War from 1754 to 1763, part of the overall European conflict the War of the Austrian Succession.

Promoted to Rear-Admiral shortly before his death in 1786, he was the father of his namesake Rear-Admiral Sir Frederick Lewis Maitland, born in 1777 and who died in 1839, and who in August of 1815 was responsible as commander of the *Bellerophon* for conveying Napoleon Bonaparte to his exile on Saint Helena.

Going back in time, to eight years before the death of John Maitland, 1st Duke of Lauderdale in 1682, and on the death of the Earl of Dundee, he was appointed in his place as Hereditary Bearer for the Sovereign of the Standard of Scotland.

In 1790, James Maitland, 8th Earl of Lauderdale, was officially granted heraldic arms as Hereditary Bearer for the Sovereign of the Standard of Scotland and Hereditary Bearer for the Sovereign of the National Flag of Scotland.

Just over 160 years later, in 1952, following

a meeting between the Earls of Lauderdale and Dundee the Lord Lyon King of Arms of Scotland – the ultimate authority on such matters – advised the Queen to confirm the Earl of Lauderdale's right as Bearer of the National Flag of Scotland, the saltire, and the Earl of Dundee as Bearer of the Royal Standard the lion rampant.

Following the death in 2008 of Sir Patrick Maitland, 17th Earl of Lauderdale and Chief of Clan Maitland and who is featured in the following chapter, his titles and honours passed to his son Ian Maitland, 18th Earl of Lauderdale and Viscount Maitland.

Thirlestane Castle, near Lauder in the Borders, remains the historic seat of the Clan Maitland chiefs.

Set in lands owned by the family since 1587 and converted into a magnificent renaissance palace for the 1st Duke of Lauderdale by the architect Sir William Brodie, extensions were carried out in 1840 by the Edinburgh architects William Burn and David Bryce that include two large wings flanking the central keep and, constructed around a central courtyard, a south wing.

Home during the Second World War to a private girls' school that had been evacuated from

Edinburgh, the castle was given into the care of a charitable trust in 1984 to ensure its preservation and, with the aid of grants from the National Heritage Memorial Fund and the Historic Buildings Council, major repairs undertaken.

With the raised ground on which it dominates the landscape known as Castle Hill and noted for attractions including an historic toy collection, fine plasterwork ceilings, porcelain, furniture and paintings, this historic seat of the chiefs of Clan Maitland is open to visitors throughout the year from the beginning of May to the beginning of October.

Yet another noted Maitland property for centuries is Lennoxlove House, about half a mile south of Haddington, East Lothian.

Once known as Lethington Castle and described by Historic Environment Scotland as "one of Scotland's most notable and ancient houses", it was built on land acquired by Robert Maitland of Thirlestane in 1345 and remained in the family until after the death of the 1st Duke of Lauderdale in 1682.

Now the seat of the Dukes of Hamilton, it boasts an important collection of portraits, porcelain, furniture and other artefacts and is open to the public during the summer months.

Chapter four:

On the world stage

Bearers of the Maitland name have achieved international fame and acclaim through a colourfully diverse range of endeavours and pursuits.

Born in 1911 in Walsall, West Midlands, **Patrick Francis Maitland**, 17th Earl of Lauderdale, was a politician, journalist and Second World War intelligence operative.

A special correspondent for *The Times* newspaper from 1939 to 1941, covering the Balkans and also for the *Washington News Chronicle*, he took an even more active role in the war while working from 1941 to 1943 as a journalist in the Pacific, New Zealand and Australia.

This saw him with the embattled U.S. Marines at Guadalcanal, while he also later abandoned his typewriter to fly a mission as a tail gunner in a B.17 bomber.

A member of the political intelligence department of the Foreign Office from 1943 until the end of the war in charge of its Yugoslav section, in 1951 he entered politics as Conservative MP (Member of Parliament) for the Scottish constituency of Lanark, holding the seat until 1959.

Succeeding to the earldom of Lauderdale in 1968, as a member of the House of Lords he served on a number of committees including, from 1974 to 1979, the Select Committee on EEC (European Economic Community) Scrutiny, while he was also a member of the Society for Individual Freedom.

President of the Church Union from 1956 to 1961 and a Fellow of the Royal Geographical Society, he died in 2008.

Through his marriage to Yugoslav-born Stanka Losanitch, he was the father of Lady Helen Olga Maitland, the journalist and Conservative politician better known as **Lady Olga Maitland**.

Born in 1944, she worked for a time as a reporter for the Fleet Street News Agency and, from 1967 to 1991, as a columnist for the *Sunday Express* newspaper.

As MP for Sutton and Cheam from 1992 to 1997, she served on a number of parliamentary committees including defence and foreign affairs, while also promoting Private Members Bills such as Offensive Weapons (1996).

The author of books including her 1989 *Margaret Thatcher: the first ten years*, in 1997 the British-based Russian journalist Yuri Sagaydak was deported after she informed the intelligence services how he had, rather naively, tried to recruit her as a spy.

From the murky world of spies to the realms of religious fantasy, **Sara Maitland** is the British author born in London in 1950.

Married to an Anglican priest from 1972 to 1993, she became a Roman Catholic following her divorce.

Her novels focus on aspects of religion, but in a much different genre her 2003 collection of short stories *Becoming a Fairy Godmother* has been described as 'a fictional celebration of the menopausal woman.'

Having worked with film director Stanley Kubrick on the 1995 *A.I. Artificial Intelligence* and the author of the short story collection *Telling Tales*, adapted for the film of the name in 2007, her daughter Polly Lee is the actress known for her work in American television series that include *Gotham*.

Her son Adam Lee is the photographer known for his series *Identity Documents*.

Born in 1839 in the Scottish town of Elgin,

Morayshire and immigrating to Canada with her father when aged 18, Mary Ann Davidson was the author of short stories, poems and hymns better known by her married name **Mary Ann Maitland**.

Her short story *Charity Ann: Founded on Facts*, first published in 1892 in *Godey's Lady's Book*, was part of the inspiration for fellow-Canadian author Lucy Maud Montgomery's 1918 children's classic *Anne of Green Gables*, while other popular works before her death in 1919 appeared in publications including *Woman's Magazine*, *Christian at Work* and *Gems of Poetry*.

Returning to the Maitland heartland of Scotland, **William Maitland** was the historian and topographer born in about 1693 in Brechin, Forfarshire.

Travelling throughout Europe as a merchant, he eventually settled in London and produced a number of illustrated works including *The History of London, from its Foundation by the Romans to the present time*, first published in 1739 and, from 1753, *The History of Edinburgh from its Foundation to the present time*.

A Fellow of the Royal Society and member of the Society of Antiquaries of London, he died in 1757.

Bearers of the Maitland name have also excelled in the highly competitive world of sport.

Of Scottish descent through his father and Samoan and Maori through his mother, **Sean Maitland** is the New Zealand rugby union player and Scottish internationalist born in 1988 in Tokoroa.

A member of the team that beat England in 2021 to take the coveted Calcutta Cup for the first time in 38 years, it is through his Glaswegian grandparents who immigrated in the 1960s that he qualifies to play for Scotland, having also represented the nation at the 2015 World Cup.

A member of the British and Irish Lions squad for the tour of Australia in 2013 and having played for clubs including Canterbury, Crusaders, Saracens and Glasgow Warriors, he is also a cousin of the New Zealand-born Australian rugby union player Quade Cooper.

Still on Antipodean shores, but in the much different sport of women's field hockey, **Clover Maitland** is the goalkeeper born in 1972 in Maryborough, Queensland.

A member of the winning team at both the 1996 and 2000 Olympics and the 1998 Commonwealth Games, she is a recipient of the

Medal of the Order of Australia (OAM) and the Australian Sports Medal.

Taking to the skies, Edward Maitland Gee was the pioneering early twentieth century aviator better known – for reasons that remain confusingly unclear – as **Edward Maitland Maitland**.

Born in 1880 in Cambridgeshire, he served during the Second Boer War of 1899 to 1902 as a lieutenant in the Essex Regiment and during the First World War of 1914 to 1918 with the Air Battalion of the Royal Engineers, Flying Corps.

He had taken up ballooning six years before the war and, in November of 1908, flew with two others in a balloon named Mammoth from Crystal Palace, London to Meeki Derevi, near Novo Aleksandrovsk in Russia – covering a distance of 1,117 miles (1,798km) in just over 36 hours.

Attached to the Balloon School at Farnborough Airfield the following year, he was awarded a Royal Aero Club Airship Pilot certificate and, in 1913, carried out from the airship Delta one of the first parachute descents.

Utilising his ballooning and airship experience, he served during the war as Officer Commanding No. 1 Squadron RFC (Royal Flying Corps) and, with the merger in 1918 of the RFC and the Royal Naval Air Service, transferred to the RAF.

In 1919 he was one of the crew aboard the airship R.34 when it completed the first transatlantic crossing, but was killed in August of 1921 when the airship R.38 broke up in mid-air over the River Humber after suffering structural failure.

One nineteenth century bearer of the Maitland name with a particularly esoteric claim to fame is the occultist, writer and humanitarian **Edward Maitland**.

Born in 1824 in Ipswich, his father was curate of St James's Chapel, Brighton, but despite this background he turned his back on established religion, declaring it to be "a tomb for the preservation of embalmed doctrines."

Graduating Bachelor of Arts from Cambridge University in 1847 and having unsuccessfully sought his fortune during the California Gold Rush and also working for a time in Australia, he returned to England in 1857.

By now a widower, his wife having died in Australia, he devoted the rest of his life to 'developing the intuitional faculty' and the formulation of a perfect system of thought and rule of life.

This was expounded in his 1873 book *By and By: an Historical Romance of the Future* and, in conjunction with the women's rights activist and fellow seeker after light Anna Kingsford, the 1875 *The Keys of the Creeds*.

A major influence on Maitland, Kingsford, born in Stratford in 1846, in addition to being steeped in mysticism was also a vegetarian, leading campaigner against vivisection and the first English woman to obtain a degree in medicine after studying in France.

In 1876 Maitland maintained he had seen an apparition of his father, who had died ten years previously, thereby convincing him that he belonged to a special 'order of the mystics'.

Claiming to be able to 'see' the spiritual side of people and believing himself to be a reincarnation of, among others, St John the Evangelist and the prophet Daniel, he was also an acquaintance of the occultist, philosopher and author Madame Helena Blavastsky, co-founder of the Theosophical Society.

Born in the Ukraine in 1831, Blavatsky was a highly influential figure in occult circles through her colourful and detailed description of how, while travelling through Tibet in search of enlightenment, she had been 'illuminated' by a group of spiritual adepts known as the Masters of the Ancient Wisdom.

But disagreement with Blavatsky, who had founded the society as a vehicle for what she had learned on her travels, led to Maitland parting company with her and founding, in collaboration with his spiritual soulmate Anna Kingsford, the alternative Hermetic Society.

Along with Kingsford, he embarked on the translation into English, from sources including ancient Greek and Hebrew texts and mysterious inscriptions, writings purported to be based on the wisdom of the legendary prophet Hermes Trismegitus.

A member of the London Spiritual Alliance and instrumental in the foundation of the Humanitarian League, he also founded the Esoteric Christian Union – through which he corresponded with Mahatma Gandhi.

It was through Maitland that Gandhi was introduced to Leo Tolstoy's 1894 book *The Kingdom of God is Within You* – which the great Indian nationalist claimed had turned him towards non-violence as a means of change.

He died in 1897, having corresponded with Gandhi up until the last.